ISBN - 13: 978-1482581423

For

Pat, Kai, Claire, Ben & Isabella

Born in the motherland of Yorkshire and then migrating south to the kingdom of Wessex, Clare Macnaughton dedicated her life to hedonism, sailing, beaches and sunshine for as long as possible then did some other stuff before she ghost wrote a battlefield memoir, called 'Immediate Response', in-conjunction with a serving Royal Marine Major, which was published by Penguin. In September 09, in the second week of sales it entered at number 9 in The Sunday Times hardback non-fiction top 10 bestseller list.

I began writing the blog called A Modern Military Mother in May 2010. This book is a compilation of the edited highlights, or cringelights. I'd like to say the best bits but, if I am being honest, it sometimes makes my toes curl when I read it back. These are my honest thoughts. Honest at the time of drafting but, of course, we grow, change, evolve and sometimes we learn new things. I am not popular and my blog has met with much aggressive and abusive opposition. Many people disagree with me. In fact, a major publishing house turned this book down because their female editorial team didn't find me very likeable. However, it has also been well received and applauded in other quarters so I know you can only please 50% of the people 100% of the time. The blog has introduced to me a world where women celebrate the opportunity to share their lives and I have met some amazing people as part of my own personal blogging journey. The digital presents many opportunities for everyone and this is my carpe diem moment.

I love the freedom my blog gives me to express myself, and long may that continue.

Thank you to Matthew Pryor and John Saddler.

Clare Macnaughton

writing as

A Modern Military Mother

Tales From

The Domestic Frontline

I have created this blog called A Modern Military Mother for women, like myself, who are married to the military and often are raising their kids alone – married, single, celibate. For the first three years of my son's life my husband was at home for, at the most, 6 months a year. It was hard for my son and my husband, as they were so disconnected from each other and our lives were so fragmented. The constant re-integration was challenging.

The idea for the blog came when I was sat on a train to London. I had got up at 7a.m., dressed the kids, given them their breakfast, dropped my 20 month old daughter at nursery, dropped my son at school, I drove from Dorset to Reading, parked at the station, and caught a train. My journey was interrupted because there was a fatality, and we were then sent back to Reading, where I had to get on another train to Waterloo. As I was waiting on the train, it slowly filled up to the gunwales. Another milly wife walked past the train window, her journey impacted by the same event. She is based in Oxfordshire and is an oncologist trying to get the Nobel Peace Prize by finding a cure for cancer. We spoke on the phone. Her husband is deployed. She had an incredibly important presentation to give in London. Her son was in childcare in Oxford and she had no back-up to collect him.

It was during this conversation I began to draft a blog. I called it A Modern Military Mother not because I am the mother of someone who is serving, but because I am mother whose parenting choices are continually impacted by my decision to marry someone in the military. In this respect I see myself as a modern military mother.

This is the beginning of a story a modern military spouse, who is a mother to her children.

I do have a very good friend who has a son who is serving and I feel her aching when he is deployed. I think it is harder for the mothers of soldiers than it is for the wives. The love I feel for my children is unconditional. The modern military mothers whose children serve endure the agony and the ecstasy of parenting more than most. I have nothing but the upmost respect and admiration for them.

A Modern Military Mother

May 16, 2010

When I first met Hagar and we were in the throes of young love. I had a perception of what a military officer's wife was like and it wasn't me.

I looked down my arrogant, young nose at those betrothed and thought I will never become one – 'no way Jose'.

To me, the military officer's spouse wore a Laura Ashley frock, twin-set and pearls, her husband's rank on her sleeve, and she arranged the flowers for the Mess in her spare time. She frequented coffee mornings, twitched her curtains, monitoring the comings and goings of her neighbours, gossiping bitchily behind their backs.

I was smoking pot, wearing skate clothes; hoody, baggy trousers, unfeasibly large trainers; writing angry, satirical, feminist verse, surfing, adventuring, pushing boundaries. The military men fascinated me with their fast chat, powerful roles and unquestioning self-assurance. We clashed delightfully and passionately; spending long evenings of red wine fuelled heated debates. Our battlefield for intellectual supremacy played out in late night games of Trivial Pursuit, Risk, Backgammon, The Name Game, and Escape From Colditz.

Time passed and Hagar proposed. I sold out feminism and accepted. The subjugation began and, nestled in the security and comfort of newlywed love, I tiptoed into the community I had readily dismissed at the beginning of our courtship. The real wives, and not the fictional versions that I had created and judged, became my friends. To be frank, there were some that fitted the stereotype but not many, and they are a breed that time and social evolution are phasing away.

In these early days, I met a senior officer's wife who came to be my friend. I almost have some weird, officer's wife crush on her because I admire her so much and I have gained so much inspiration from her. By profession she is an Occupational Psychotherapist, so she, like me, loves to observe, dissect, question and ultimately try to understand why and how we are who we are.

One night under the domination of the red wine mistress, we began a conversation that four years on we have yet to finish. What does the modern military wife look like? Who is she? How does she function in the modern military landscape? We both challenge the stereotype by who we are as people and yet the stereotype still pervades the military culture that we inhabit.

In our red wine fuelled state, we dreamed a dream; to create a conference to gather modern military spouses and partners so that we can challenge the stereotype, but also to find who we are, how our lives are constructed and what we need to help support our spouses and each other.

Hagar's fantasy family

May 25 2010

It's been a while since Hagar's been deployed on ops and as I prepare for its coming I think back to the challenges we have previously faced.

The thing about the war in Afghanistan is that it is a violent, feudal battlefield, but his life is ordered and structured. Hagar goes to war and he can focus solely on the job at hand. They eat, sleep, plan, brief, execute, de-brief, eat, sleep and maybe they'll work out, read and shoot the shit with each other. Life is laid out for them in a structured, co-ordinated manner. Hagar walks into a room to give a brief. The room is silent and listens to what he has to say until he has finished speaking.

He takes with him photos of us, his family, in still, poised poses. Good pictures, where we are happy, beautiful statues of perfections. He pines and aches for us as he remembers fondly the moments he played dinosaur battles on the living room floor with The Grenade, our 6-year-old son. He imagines me cooking up a warm, homely, veritable feast like a domestic goddess, keeping the home fires burning, laughing gaily as he speaks and celebrating the Utopian banter of our perfect marriage.

When he returns home, all suntanned, dusty and crunchy from the sand, after the initial moments of euphoria of being re-united are over, normal life kicks in. The memories of his fantasy family are shattered and he is faced with his real family. The Grenade is whining - ear drum shattering whines - because something that he deemed essential to his very being has been denied to him. The house is chaotic, strewn with toys, dinner is not served and the bubba is screaming. He starts to talk to me about something that barely interests me, maybe something mechanical and military like. I start thinking about something else distracted. He looks at me and says; 'I am talking to you and you are not listening,' and I reply, 'Yes, I know but it's not that interesting and I am your wife, not one of your crew and I reserve the right to be bored, switch off, interrupt and think about something else, entirely irrelevant and disconnected to your conversation.'

Sometimes it's easy and simpler to go to war. Hagar knows where he is at war. Home is messy, noisy, chaotic and full of hormonal, evolving people who don't follow the rules. I know he loves us and we love him, but there is more than just distance between war and home. This is why the re-integration back in is always complicated as we all learn how to be around each other again.

Competitive perfection

June 6, 2010

On Friday night Hagar and I were watching a programme called something like 'Killing the Red Baron'. In it were two ex-Fast Jet Pilots, who said that all pilots, in their nature, were competitive. Hagar agreed and then decanted his day. He had just returned from the Air Medical Training Wing, where he had spent the day in various states of hypoxia. He and his pilot chum climbed into a big steel hypobaric cylinder with 10 seats and a sealed door and were taken to a simulated height of 17,500ft with equivalent pressure. At 10,000ft they took their oxygen masks off. They then climbed to 17,500ft and spent 30 minutes at that altitude. During the 30 minutes they were given a series of texts and increasing complex diagrams to copy to assess the slow onset of hypoxia and understand the physical impact on the body. He and his chum embarked on an unspoken competition to see who could complete most sentences and diagrams as perfectly as possible, before they, potentially, passed out. Neither mentioned it, but they both knew the challenge was on.

This competitive perfection spills into our domestic life. Everything about Hagar's training centres around Time On Target (TOT), arriving at the objective as the clock turns zero – this is what success looks like to Hagar. I operate in TOT plus 10-

15 minutes, which drives Hagar insane. But at the same time in civvy street, it's impolite to ring the doorbell the second the clock turns onto the hour when arriving at a social function.

For me, the non-military infidel wife, I try to somehow strike a balance between the paradox of our lives and beliefs. Hagar and I are opposites and sometimes it really works, and sometimes it really doesn't - but it keeps us on our toes. It has been pointed out to me that I seem to have a love-hate relationship with the military, and it's true, I really do. It's complex and genuinely unresolvable. It's part of the dichotomy that is our life, so we just bumble through it as best we can.

Like I said, this competitive perfection does spill over into our domestic life and I, too, am fiercely competitive, so I find myself getting sucked in, when really I should know better and walk away. But the yo-yo continues and it isn't changing anytime soon, so the internal battle continues on.

A couple of years ago, when The Grenade was a mere 18 months old, I was working as PR Manager for solo yachtsman Mike Golding, managing his PR while he sailed non-stop solo around the globe on a his 60ft Open 60, Ecover, in the Vendee Globe 2004.

It was Christmas and the race was around halfway. The Grenade was an insomniac and Mike had been at sea for around 40 days, so life was pretty full on. We had been invited to a mince pie drinks party by another military couple with a flock of other military couples also invited. But there was a twist – it was going to be a mince pie bake off. I very foolishly thought this was actually meant as a tongue cheek, slightly camp gesture. Each of the wives was expected to bring their finest examples of mince pie bakery.

In the midst of an intense media campaign, we were head-to-head with Ellen Macarthur's solo record attempt and sailing media airtime was in short supply. Coupled with the 18 months of intense sleep deprivation due to The Grenade's mania, rather than saying, 'No', I stepped up to the plate. Thirty minutes prior to departure, I cut up some filo pastry (that I had bought and defrosted earlier) into squares, shoved in a tea spoon of mincemeat (that I had bought earlier), turned into a parcel, repeat 20 times, bake for 10 minutes at gas mark 6, (I cook everything at gas mark 6) and dusted with icing sugar. Stick on plate, bundle Grenade and Hagar into car, attend drinkypoos.

Now, Hagar and I, we were one of the first of this little military clique to squeeze out offspring and quite frankly we had produced a lively one. We arrived at the party and The Grenade immediately curled one down in his nappy.

After 18 months, I was a pro at the super whippy, minimal

impact, poo change and so, in lightning speed, in a far corner of the kitchen, I did a power-charged nappy change, to the very sour tutts of all childless, young wifelet attendees and the whispers of 'really, you should do that elsewhere'. (Interestingly, in the last month, two of the tutters have squeezed out sprogs and both changed their offspring's turd filled nappies on my living room floor without so much as batting an eyelid – how things have moved on. I guess it's just one of the disadvantages of producing early).

The mince pies are produced and to my horror it appears that this is not some tongue-in-cheek mince pie gag but a very serious competition. The women are instructed to stay in the kitchen, whilst the men folk adjourn to the dining room to judge the mince pies, with a set judging criteria. It turns out that one wifelet has got her granny's best recipe and this is actually her fourth batch, so intent on victory was she!

I am pretty horrified at the hideousness of the occasion. I can't help thinking 'what is going on?' The judges return and the results are announced; the filo pastry parcel pies are 2nd. The Grenade starts to cause destruction beyond what is acceptable and I have to publish the evening polls on the Vendee Globe, so we take our leave and head home.

Thinking about Jerry Hall's famous quote; 'My mother said it was simple to keep a man, you must be a maid in the living room, a cook in the kitchen and a whore in the bedroom.'

I mumbled something along the lines of; "next year instead of mince pies, why don't the husbands just take it in turns to fuck each one of us" – a worthier attribute than our bake-ability, but I don't think anyone heard, as they were all twittering lard and flour.

When we get home The Grenade chucked his ring up all over the hall floor, and in the midst of this I received a text telling me that after some deliberation, it was decided that the filo pastry parcels were disqualified as I bought the pastry. 'Arrrgghhh!!!' – As I was up to my elbows in baby puke, I couldn't give a flying fuck.

Six years on we are the new folks on the block in our current quarters. The front of the house is south facing and everyone on our street has a little bench in front of their kitchen window, a little personal expression of who they are. When we moved into a new military quarter on a new 'military patch' (the collective noun for military housing estate), I swore to Hagar I would not be swayed and that we would not be joining the bench club. But six weeks in and the 'keeping up with the Jones's' competitive brain cell is squeaking naughty thoughts into my head...'buy bench' it's saying. "Aaaarghhh!!!' I have resisted so far but I am not sure how much longer I can ignore it for. This is part of the paradox; I am the conforming rebel – the battle rages on.

Where were you when Diana died?

June 8, 2010

It was 3am on August 26th 1997 and I was lying drunk on the floor of Stasia's cottage, in the heart of Colonies, in the gutters of majestic Edinburgh. It was a particularly average summer, warm, humid but mainly overcast. The night air felt thick with the weight of intoxication around my face and the smoke danced languidly above my head. I was swirling in a happy place, sharing the shadows of lamplight with my friends and giggling at the past evening's events. The radio was wooing us in the distance with cheesy eighties love songs. When suddenly a voice pierced icily into our warm haze:

"News just in – The Princess of Wales has been involved in a car crash in Paris. It is unknown at this time the severity of the accident, but her situation is thought to be critical." The news landed into the room with a jolt.

I sat up; the room shot round like a waltzer. "Did you hear that Stasia? Did everyone hear that, or was I tripping? Princess Diana has been in a car accident. Shit! I can't believe it. Weird."

I slumped back, waiting for the room to stop spinning.

Barry, Stasia, Figgis and I sat up, numbed by the news, the enormity of it slowly dawning on us. Quietly we all muttered questions, too wasted to make any sense of what we had heard.

Figgis got up, turned the radio off and put a tape on to prevent another reality intrusion; but the warmth of the womb that had nurtured us had been coldly cut open, and it was time to end the night with sleep. In the morning, we turned the radio on and learnt that the Princess of Wales had in fact died in the crash and that it wasn't a fuggy, drunken dream but a real time shared experience. Significant only because we shared that moment together, and so, when people ask; "Do you remember what you were doing when Princess Diana died?" I think fondly of my three friends, who were so instrumental in shaping my life, and whose journeys have now taken us all down separate paths.

Later that year, on 20th October 1997, I met Hagar on a blind date in Edinburgh set up by Stasia. I had clean snapped in two my fibula and tibia in my ankle, whilst on a speed boat watching the start of the 1997 Whitbread round the world yacht race. I was thrown over to the side as we went awkwardly over a wave, causing me to land badly on my ankle. I was lodging with my gran Betty, in York, healing. This marked the beginning of the journey from who I was then, to who I am now.

I hate housework!

June 15, 2010

It's tedious, monotonous and infinite! I resent the fact that Hagar doesn't do as much as me and has somehow managed to morph a relationship founded on equality into one of segregated conjugal roles. How did this happen? At the same time, I know that I lead a privileged existence and inside my soul I should be pleased to serve my family and create the nest that they all need to function to the optimum. Yet, I can't help it – it really pisses me off that it's me that has to be the slave!

My gran, Betty, was the guiding light of my life. She was one of 14 children. She grew up in a country village near Peterborough. My great-grandfather was a drunk and gambled his father's fortune away. Gran lived in a tumbledown cottage and she and her siblings would have to collect the family's water from a pump in the middle of the village square. At 14, she left home and moved to Coventry to live in lodgings with her sister Pearl. She worked as a secretary to an army officer.

At 16 she met my grandfather, Ginge (a redhead – the clue is in the nickname). He had been dragged up working on the docks of the River Ouse in York. His father had been murdered with a docker's claw for his wage packet.

He slept rough around York docks until he was 15. When the war came he was called up and enlisted in the RAF as a rear gunner. According to my very uncharitable father, he was a big boozer and spent most of the war in the brig for drinking offences, hence the reason he managed to survive a role where death was almost guaranteed.

After the war, Ginge and Betty married, and moved to York, where they were issued a council house at 49 Tenent Road. This is where they lived until they both died. They had four children. My mother was the eldest and born in 1947. Life at 49, as it was always known through my raising, was pretty turbulent. Gran and Grandad had come from nothing and they had nothing. The house was furnished with filth, orange boxes and love. Grandad was now working at Rowntrees as a painter and decorator; a job he held until he retired. Ginge was a drinker – he loved his booze. He could open his throat and pour the amber nectar down his neck in voluminous quantities. His greatest achievement was that he could drink a pint in under 5 seconds.

He could be found in The White Rose most nights, drinking and playing dominos. My mum quite often would have to pull him and his bike out of the hedge in the morning and make sure he got to work on time. Betty kept the home fires burning, stoically and cheerfully – held together by tots of brandy and many fags.

He was a womaniser as well. When Ginge's fancy women would turn up at the back door, Gran would shriek, "Gin-ner! There's a women here says you are leaving me. Are you going?"

"No Bette," would be the sheepish response.

"Did you hear that?" Gran would spit at the doorstep dalliance, "Now sling yer hook."

Betty's darkest day was when my mother died at the age of 26. She could never speak of it. She put it in a secure vault and buried her grief deep inside her soul, never to be unlocked. In fact it took until I was 18 years old before she could put a photo of my mum, amongst the collection of family memorabilia, framed and set amidst the vast array of porcelain birds.

Through this rollercoaster of a life, my gran served her family and her grandkids and others as well. She cleaned, washed and ironed – singing terribly, crooning. She fed every stray dog and child in Tenent Road. Many kids sought refuge from life at Betty's house. You would never know who would be living there and for how long. She couldn't bear to see a child in pain.

She worked as a barmaid in The Mania Bar at York Station Hotel. She was straight out of Andy Cap – lacquered blonde hair, bright pink, powder and paint, black skirt, white shirt, with an ample cleavage and killer patent leather heels.

How she worked shifts in these shoes, I have no idea. On day shifts, she would sneak me in and hide me from the management. Whenever the bosses came down I would scuttle behind the crisp boxes under the bar and wait for them to leave. My reward for silence and stillness was 10p for the fruit machine that would often multiply magically into a £1.

All she did was work, smoke, sing, dance and celebrate life. She waited on all of us. She said she was born to serve. 'You come to my house to relax', she would say to me. She was proud to serve her family. Her house was a real refuge. My refuge. I called it the 'bosom'. The bosom of Betty.

Betty Smith

Like a shining star,

a blooming flower,

early morning and a face that is sour.

She can be bright and gay,

like a sunny day.

She has a twinkle in her eye,

and a sparkle in her smile,

she is loaded with love,

she is armed with style.

With a life full of pain,

it is from her that I gain,

that at the end of the day,

when it is all said and done

and push comes to shove,

there is no one like Betty,

she defines the word love.

I think of my gran and the spirit she inspired within me. I give myself a little pep talk. I am blessed to have such a wonderful gift with my life, two gorgeous children, the handsome Hagar, a beautiful nest to raise my kids and yet no matter how much I try I still can't help hating housework. It's so boring and pointless! When Hagar comes home and I have cooked a fabulous home-cooked meal, with fresh ingredients, from scratch and then I end up doing the washing up and putting the kids to bed as well, the nagging 'I am not born to serve' battle unleashes itself. I blame Thatcher! She was a false icon – she had staff and a millionaire husband! I need me some of those. It's no good, I can't help it – I hate housework. Right, that said I have to go and make the beds. The battle continues on.

'Someday I'm going to do and say everything I want to do and say, and if people don't like it I don't care.' – Scarlett O'Hara

Ginge

July 7, 2010

I upset my Aunty Pat, with my 'I Hate Housework' post. She felt that my poor Grandad, aka Ginge, received a bit of a raw deal and that I didn't touch upon the things about him that made him truly wonderful and only looked at some of the darker sides. I deeply loved my Grandad too, he was an equal part of the rock built foundation of love that was 49 Tenent Rd which gave me the security to grow into a loved child.

Those pre-feminist black and white days of the 50s and 60s, in the industrial North, and the film, 'Saturday Night, Sunday Morning' culture personified by Albert Finney, was part of that time.

It was after Grandad died that those days came out to air in the back room, next to the gas fire, sipping strong Yorkshire tea, cup after cup,

'Ooh your Grandad could be a right sod!' said Betty as she spun the tales of those early beginnings.

But the Grandad I knew as a child was gentle, kind, happy, simple man, who waited for me at the gate of 49, with his arms stretched wide and his knees bent, as I ran as fast my chubby little legs could carry me, into his strong, swooping arms and spun into candescent laughter. He was always waiting for me in his banger at the station when my train arrived. He always made me bacon sandwiches in the morning.

Betty made the best Yorkshire puddings in the world, as big as dinner plates. Grandad would always eat them as a starter, saturated in gravy. It was fixed, firm rule of Yorkshire pudding eating etiquette. This, the traditional way to eat them. A pudding as a starter, only in Yorkshire!

I can see him now, sat in his chair in the back room, doing The Daily Express crossword, waiting to collect, or deliver me, or make me a cup of tea. When I was young, he would wrap tinfoil around a finger on each hand and sing me a song,

> *"Two little dickie birds, sitting on a wall, one name Peter, one named Paul,"*

> *"Fly away Peter' with slight of hand, one piece tinfoil would vanish,*

> *"Fly away Paul,"* whoosh there would go the second. I would marvel at the trickery.

> *"Come back Peter,"* whoosh, there was the tinfoil.

> *"Come back Paul."* And the other piece too.

It was so funny and clever. I thought he was the best Grandad ever.

Love Endurance

June 17, 2010

A big chopper

Up, up, into the sky, the juddering rumble of the spinning rotators.

If only Leonardo had explained why,

Those circling blades made it fly.

Does anyone know just what makes it go?

Up, up into the sky the juddering rumble of the spinning rotators.

I knew that I wanted to spend the rest of my life with Hagar, ironically, when he went on his first deployment for 8 weeks. It wasn't even war – it was just an exercise. He spent 8 weeks on HMS Ocean. I can remember feeling like we were being severed. I knew that, if I could feel this much pain as I pined, I must truly love him, otherwise I wouldn't care.

When we met he was stationed at RAF Aldergrove in Northern Ireland. He was a Puma navigator.

He worked 3 weeks in Northern Ireland and then would come home for a week at a time. I was wrapped deliciously in the intoxication of young, passionate love.

Time slowly passes

If only the passing grains of time
Would flow fast then slow.
Quickly when we are divided,
Slowly when we are united.

A planted seed of passion.
A one week a month ration.
Our first kiss made my insides glow,
My legs weak, my knees go.

I tumbled into your strong embrace
And immersed myself in your face.
Wet kisses like silk,
A warm sweet nectar of honey and milk.
Time passes, days past flow.

A candle burns deep inside me,
Each second I feel its flame grow.

Don't leave me.
Hug me, squeeze me,
Baby I love you, don't ever let go.

I miss the innocence and passion of our youthful love, but it's nice to reflect on it here, now, as we prepare to be severed again. The children are a distraction. They make the time pass faster. We can't indulge in each other with the same intensity anymore but I am delighted that we once did.

Original Sin

June 21, 2010

Hagar looked lovingly across the table and sighed; "I was going to say 'I love you', but what came out was 'you bitch, you've ruined my life'."

This is a constant joke between us – ha ha ha! How we laugh! The children are revolting. Life is demanding and somehow, the tempo and pressure has gone off the scale, and we are like hamsters on a wheel just trying to keep up with it.

It reminds me of Basil Fawlty:

Basil: *Oh, it's my fault is it? I thought it was your fault for falling asleep or Manuel's fault for not waking you, and all the while it was my fault. Oh, it's so obvious now I've seen the light! Well, I must be punished then, mustn't I? (slaps his bottom) You're a naughty boy Fawlty, don't do it again!*

I remember a male friend of mine, who had just been dumped, calling all women 'snakes with tits.' The notion being that women are poisonous evil, vipers designed to fuck up a man's day.

The Grenade had a summer fete at school where he had to enter an Egg Cresshead; an eggshell filled with wet cotton wool and cress seeds which grow into cress hair. We very diligently grew our cresshead egghead and then knowing that The Grenade is not a detail kind of kid, we racked our brains to try and find a concept that he could actually deliver himself. I am not one of those parents who does their child's homework for them. I get really annoyed when I get homework from school that is very clearly for me and not for my child, and also knowing that we could get potentially sucked in to a massive, parent homework bully off. My little Johnny is not going to be made to look like the child he is in real life – step in competitive parents. I am afraid my little boy is left to battle out his strengths and weaknesses, with support of course, but I did my homework years ago and that was plenty thanks.

I chose the theme Garden of Eden. He was loving his clay modelling at that moment so I instructed him to rustle up a tree of life, a serpent (actually based on an anaconda, The Grenade's favourite serpent) and an apple.

We did art-direct the apple a little. Hagar took the bite. I suggested the white clay on the inside. Hagar and I had two egg cups, a naked from the waist down man and a woman that we had painted for each other at a ceramics shop. It was our valentine's gift to each other one year. It was childish but also, we thought it was funny and, again, it was before children, when I hadn't 'ruined his life'!

(To be honest, these are the only egg cups we have in the house so it was our best option to somehow incorporate them into the theme. 'Light bulb moment' Garden of Eden. Perfect.)

In order to cover the rude bits, I bought some baby spinach leaves and stuck them over the offending genitalia with non-toxic glue.

Having created the Garden of Eden we instructed him to draw on the eggs and by some miracle, some could say it was divine intervention, he drew the faces which accurately reflected the mood in the garden, post Eve's bite of the apple. Hurrah! Egghead fete entry, tick! So just in case, I decided that I would explain the theme to the Grenade so that he could, at least, if interrogated, demonstrate some working knowledge of what was going down on that ill-fated day.

Right here goes – so God created man in his own form, then from his rib, he creates a women called Eve, but says, 'whatever, you do don't eat any apples from the Tree of Life.'

While Adam is not looking a serpent comes along and says, 'eat the apple, you know you want to, apples are yummy.' Eve eats apple. God is angry – I said, 'don't eat the apple!' and sentences 'Adam to hard labour and Eve gets childbirth.' Oh I see, so it's all our fault is it! Adam looks at Eve and says, 'I meant to say I love you but what came out was, you bitch, you've ruined my life!'

It's started

June 25, 2010

Hagar is back in the cockpit and with it starts the unpredictability of our life. Big deep breath and the 'super chilled, I can handle anything you throw at me' head has to be dusted off. The job comes first, that is the fact of life that I never take on, or contest. The function of the support we give is that we never question the job and we work around it.

I had a fairly busy day yesterday, with a bit of juggling. The Menace (my 2-year-old daughter) was with her childminder, The Grenade was at school. I had few press releases to get out, some domestic admin, and at 5.30 p.m. I needed to be at the school for a parent briefing from the head teacher, and then at 7.30 p.m. I had confirmed that I would attend a Ladies Dinner Night at the Mess. A fellow wifelette's husband had been posted and this would be our last opportunity to catch up before she is catapulted into another county. Hagar was flying but had said he would be back by 7 p.m.

He knew that he needed to be back so I could go out and there were no issues, it was simply a matter of co-ordinating the timings.

At 10am, I received a call; "the cab's gone tits." (translation = the helicopter is broken)

"Right." I paused.

"I haven't left yet, the ETA is pushed back. I won't be home until 8.30pm."

"Right," I said.

"I'll call if it changes." Click.

O.K. Now I am re-jiggling in my head. I text my friend, who lives in quarters located on the RAF station. We live off base. By this I mean we live in military quarters that are 20 minutes drive from the RAF air base. It is a mixed patch for all services; Navy, Army and RAF. These houses are used as overflow quarters when there are no dwellings available at the work location of the serving member. I am thinking that it might be best to collect The Menace at 5 p.m. and bring her to the parent briefing because it seems unfair to pick her up at 7 p.m., and then dump her with my friend's husband, who I will call The Bear. He will now be juggling 5 kids (including my 2).

So instead I'll drag The Menace along to the briefing, which will make it marginally stressful; newbie mum (me, we have just been posted, so we are the new kids on this school circuit) flying solo at a parent gig, with rogue 2-year-old and The Grenade leaping around the school playing fields like a gazelle on speed. I am not changing the childminder yet though, so the text is a holding plan B, to milly friend, who will be flexible without being irritated by any further change to the plan.

'Mate, Hagar not back until 8pm any chance The Bear will watch my kids for an hour from 7.30pm when he gets back to station. Or even that I come to yours and handover to save me an hour. xxx"

She replied: 'Sure that will be fine, bring them to us. See you at 7.30 x'

At 3.30pm, the phone rang.

"Hi, it's me. The cab is still US," pronounced Yoo Ess – translation – the helicopter is still broken, "but we are scheduled to lift (take off) at 5.30 p.m., but I won't be back until 10 p.m."

"Well, call me if you are lifting then."

"I can't call you if we are lifting because I'll be sat in the seat," translation – the seat of the cockpit and if we go, we go. "I'll call you at 5.30 p.m. if we don't go. It's the best I can do."

"How optimistic are you feeling about going?" I asked.

"I think we'll go, it's only a box." Sorry no translation, that's all of I got and I wasn't looking for a mechanical analysis.

Click.

Now, I am thinking, 'Shit! 10 p.m. That changes everything. Now I need a babysitter instead.' I called a friend whose daughter babysits and she didn't answer. Do I dump the kids on The Bear on the pretext that it's an 8.30 p.m. pick up, so that it's 10.30 p.m. collection and just load him up with DVD material that'll keep them both occupied? Fortunately, my kids are insomniacs and it has its benefits – they don't need sleep in the ways some kids do.

At 4.30 p.m. I get myself ready for my parent briefing dinner/night out and rustle up an outfit that can carry both events. I throw on some make-up and start gathering PJ's and DVDs. I am opting to leave them with The Bear and see how it plays out. Experience has taught me never to set your life by the timings.

4.45 p.m. the phone rings; "We've shit canned it. I can pick The Menace up at 5.30pm." This means that they have decided not to go.

'Phew!' I ring the childminder and let her know that Hagar will collect The Menace at 5.30 p.m. I text my friend, 'Cab U.S. no babysitter required.'

I think, as I jump in the car and head to school for my briefing, 'it's started, the beginning of the chaos and no control.'

Who wears the daddy pants?

June 27, 2010

I have always been a bit of raging feminist. I am free spirit at heart, with dreams of eco-living, so being married to the military often causes clashes of perspective. When I met Hagar, I wrote passionately about retaining my independence of thought. I often say, much to Hagar's chagrin, that I only married him because of the military. The perks are better. It's not that I don't love him, but I was never interested in getting married and, to some extent, by getting married I sold feminism out. I realise it now and didn't see it coming. But hey, we live with the consequences of our choices and I don't regret getting married (Hagar will be relieved!).

Our relationship was founded on equality and we were, at the beginning, equal partners. We have one rule, which still stands, called the 'Yes/No' Rule. The basic premise is that before any decision is taken both parties have to say 'yes', a no is an instant refusal and if either party feels passionate about the choice, then it's rock, paper, scissors. Outcome determined, end of – no debate. This is still in play and really works for us.

I noticed a change in the equality shift after the birth of The Grenade. I was on maternity leave from work and Hagar started expecting me to do things because I was at home that, in the past, we had always shared. It's a difficult debate to have, because obviously I was on maternity leave, so to some extent it was fair that I picked up this workload. He started using language, such as; I was the 'primary childcarer'. Interesting, because I thought we did this together. He was shedding the equality like a snake sloughs its skin and, once the skin was gone, the burden of responsibility fell further onto my shoulders. Hagar has the best get of jail free card because he is in the military and the military is his mistress. She top trumps any gig that I can muster so, once he started shedding the burden, it became mine and I knew that I could never hand it back.

As I became responsible for the domestic admin, a new war was waged between us. Who was in charge in the relationship? Once we had children and were creating our own family values, Hagar, who was from a textbook family, began emulating the family childhood from which he was raised. I, not from a textbook family, constantly question our roles and how they are delivered. I run a fairly tight ship because I keep many balls in the air; I have patterns, systems, everything has its place. It's how I cope. Hagar who is dominated at work by his military mistress, understandably wants to let his hair down at home, but at the same time still call the shots. This is where we conflict because I am happy to do stuff for Hagar.

We are a partnership, but I determine the priority of my day not him. Yesterday, when Hagar was nipping my head, because I hadn't done something he asked, I snapped.

"I am not your fucking PA. I don't work for you. Yes, I said I would do it and I will, but right now, it's not a priority. If it's so fucking important you can always do it yourself. You are not in charge!" I screamed at him.

Hagar thinks he is in charge. As far as he's concerned, he wears the daddy pants. At least, he has the decency to say it so that I can tell him to 'fuck off', but the military is the mistress of us all and she top trumps everything, so I am bound by the situation. It makes for continuous dinnertime debate, and it keeps the passion alive, as the war is waged between us.

Night Stalking

June 30, 2010

In top trumps terms, the words 'I am night flying x number of nights this week' are the most annoying. This is because night flying means that Hagar has to stay up late, mainly watching a US TV show, called Sons of Anarchy, or surfing the Internet. He gets to lie-in, and then leave later in the day the next day and then come home after the kids have gone to bed. This is all in the name of crew-rest and it's a hard pill to swallow. What about wife rest? I could do with a bit of night flying.

Now, I also happen to know that many soldiers don't get crew-rest, they just soldier on, exhausted. Obviously, it would be a different matter if Hagar was to crash and he was operating outside of the mandatory crew-rest flying parameters. The regulations are something like, typically, a 12-hour duty days for rotary wing and 14-hour duty days for fixed wing with 8-10 hour rest periods in between.

The night flying has begun. The kids and I are learning how to hang without Hagar. We are gradually learning one day at a time how to be separated again.

Early exits – before children

July 3, 2010

He closed the door behind him as he left early on a spring morning. I heard the latch click and his feet stomp away. The gate opened, and he neglected to shut it properly and I knew it would tap gently in the wind, like Chinese water torture, forcing me to rouse out of my bed and skip barefooted down the path to close it. The coldness of the concrete would burn my feet and turn them into blocks of ice.

I lay snug in the duvet, tasting the shadows of his kisses on my lips, delaying the moment of execution. I heard the car door slam. I could visualise him settling into his seat, pulling the seat belt across his broad shoulders, placing his key in the ignition, his strong fingers turning it to start the engine. The engine fired and I heard the gentle throb of the motor as his car pulled away – taking Mr Rabbit to war, or to whatever. Taking him away again – for four weeks – it's not that long.

It was different this time – no contact, no phone calls, no emails, he was going undercover, underground, into isolation or something else, something military, a language I didn't talk. A language I didn't want to talk – it wasn't my name on the commission.

Tap, tap, tap, tap – the gate constantly reminded me of his absence, echoing around the garden, round the bedroom. The house felt like a cold, dank empty cave and I felt warm and safe under the covers. Protected from the grim reality of being alone. Married, single and celibate.

I couldn't hide forever and eventually the tapping of the gate drove me to distraction. I got up and felt the chill of the day envelope me. Covered in goose pimples, I grabbed my dressing gown and wrapped it around my shoulders. With a lightning pace I whipped through the house and down the path, to secure the gate. Once it was shut I turned on my heel and sprinted back inside, up the stairs, throwing myself back into bed, where I could still feel the warmth of the imprint of my body on the sheets. Pulling the duvet up to my nose, I lay there waiting to melt back into the luxury of sleep. But it was no good, my cold feet took over, and no matter how much I tried to ignore it I knew that the moment of comfort had gone, and that I was now wide awake and up. I looked at the clock – 8 a.m. I was going to have to get up and face the day.

The fairytales I had heard as a child never covered what happened in 'Happily Ever After' once you had landed the prince. I had married my prince charming; a stunningly handsome RAF helicopter pilot, who had rescued me when I had a broken leg and nothing to smile about.

He had picked me up in his arms and we had rode off into the sunset on his dashing steed. We set up home in an average, military three up, two down semi, in a wood lined cul-de-sac on the edge of Surrey, where I baked homemade bread and got really fat. This was before children, ageing and time. This is a tale of our early departures, some scene setting. I am more used to it now but I still feel like a half of a whole when he's away. We are starting to write him off in our planning, counting him as not here. The work up to war is beginning and Hagar is preparing. I am preparing too, getting organised, working out what I need to cope, to keep me sane and to be kind to myself so I can raise the kids well, with managed stress.

I don't like war but I have no choice. I wouldn't have chosen this war. However, the reality of our lives is war - whether I like it or not. Sometimes I feel desperately supportive, and other times I hold my breath and wish I was on a beach somewhere free as a bird, partying.

A soldier died yesterday, not a friend, not someone we knew, but someone a couple of handshakes away. The tempo of operations in Afghanistan is increasing and he needs to be ready, to be the best he can be. He wants to go. I want him to go because that is what he wants. It's not what you think. It's his job and, I believe, he is the best of the best. Our country needs him and he's ready and willing to step up to the plate – right now it's where he belongs.

Don't feel sorry for us; we don't need your pity, we need your support. I am writing this blog to help you understand our journey. Support the families and support the troops by believing in us, and not looking the other way. They want to win. It's all about victory for the serving and I want them to win. The British military may not be the best funded, we might not have the best kit, but we have the best serviceman because as a nation we have a stubborn tenacity, guile, resilience and fight. We adapt, we are flexible and we push boundaries. Please support us, don't pity us. Don't let those lives be sacrificed in vain.

Bumholes

July 5, 2010

My 7 year old son, asked me last night, "Mummy, do you and daddy ever snog?'"

"Absolutely not!" I replied.

"Why not?" he asked.

"Because his breath smells of bumholes," I said. Following which, he properly cracked up.

I love it that he thinks the word 'bumholes' is so funny. To be honest, I think it's really funny too and I love getting him to say it, because he always cracks up. When he is pulling a strop I become very stern and say, "Right, that's it come here. How dare you be so grumpy. I order you to say 'bumholes' without laughing." Now, this is a nigh on impossible task for a 7 year old boy.

I can't believe that I am allowed to parent a child, it seems insane, but it has its moments of preciousness that I love. Sometimes, I am a very naughty parent. I love the fact that I can tell my son what to do and he'll do it (if I am lucky) without questioning me. For example, when my husband is bellowing at me from another room in the house, to instruct me to do something I can't be bothered to attend to, I summon my wee man over.

"Do me a favour and go and tell daddy he blows goats," I sigh wistfully.

"Ok mummy," he says, and off he trips.

While I am lazing on the sofa, I hear this little voice saying to Hagar, wherever his bellowing has come from, "Daddy, Mummy says you blow goats, but I actually think you blow baby elephants."

Oh, how the winter evenings fly by.

Girls V Girls

July 11, 2010

I have to confess that I don't really understand the unspoken rules of Girldom and I pay heavily for getting it wrong. A friend said to me that she thinks it's because my mum died when I was 2 years old and I wasn't raised by a matriarch but instead by a man, who raised me as a boy. I don't have the same insecurity radar that, I think, girls pick up from their mothers, or even, that instinctive spidey-sense, for social situations. I am definitely a bit thick when it comes to reading the signs - 'Why are you kicking me under the table Hagar?' But as I get older and I focus on raising my family and shaping my future I realise that it isn't as important as it might have appeared in the past.

I believe that women should look out for each other, but I don't think that all women feel the same. This is when they draw handbags, stick out their claws and let the bitch-fest begin. In the mummy blogosphere, there has been a bit of handbag bashing and hair pulling. I don't know the detail, but what I can tell is that there is female power struggle going on about who is head hen in the henhouse.

In the milly community, it can be a hair pulling and scratchy place as well. It's full of cliques and girl gang uppery. I see this often in the UK millies, whereas I think in the US they have a greater sense of community than we do here in Blighty. I think it's because the US serving do longer deployments of over 12 months. The days of Raj are over and I think the dependent wife, who filled her day finding out which butcher provided the best cuts and wearing her husband's rank on her sleeve, are phasing out. However, as the tempo of ops increases, I think there is a need for greater solidarity amongst the community and the millies.

In my own personal circles there are a group of millies who look down their noses at those who live on patch (the married patch, AKA military quarters) and think they are superior. This group of people were really close friends of mine years ago, but dumped me when The Grenade was born because he didn't follow the baby instruction book and he wasn't a sleeper. We were the first to have kids and they blamed me for not being strict enough with him. I didn't know what was going on. Hagar was constantly deployed, lack of a matriarch and baby train wreck-head from intense sleep deprivation meant I was in a fog. Rather than supporting me, they ostracised me and judged my parenting skills. It turns out that The Grenade has mild dyspraxia and maybe a dose of ADHD.

While this was happening a new Queen Bee joined the scene and she had an axe to grind with me. She didn't like me and she wanted to boot me out of the group. She was incredibly well versed in female manipulation. She was an expert at working the henhouse, unlike me, an almost homogenous rooster. This decorative hen was a master at flattery and she wooed the other hens, who had had enough of the insomniac Grenade disrupting their dinner parties. So the expulsion began.

But there is a twist. I thought that it was just your bog standard, bitchy, backstabbing; she is wearing the wrong shoes, type dumping, but no. It turned out the Queen Bee had a dark secret. I learnt about it only after I was given the 'radio silence' by the gang by the other girl in the tryst, a close friend and ally of mine. A secret that she wanted no one to know. A secret that I didn't know and would never had known had they not expelled me.

I just got dumped recently by an old school friend who I had known since I was 11. She sent me the 'Dear John' in an email, in the same email that she was thanking me for the wedding gift I had just sent her.

One of her issues is that I don't tell her what she wants to hear and it drives her mad. She wants me to say 'poor you' but I am saying, 'keep fighting' and it winds her up. She wanted pity and I gave her support. Really, it didn't need to be so terminal – it could have been an honest, candid conversation and this is the world of Girldom that I don't understand, because I am a 'what you see is what you get' person. I am no angel, I am a difficult, stubborn, old goat and maybe it's difficult to be my friend. By the way, she kept the gift.

Women have enough to contend with just being, raising kids, living with men and managing our lives without other women getting all bitchy and stabbing them in the back. It's a lonely path and it has cost me dearly, but now that I am older I can handle the solitude and at least I know in my heart and my soul that I am doing the right thing. However, if you have it sussed, and you would care to share the girl rulebook with me, then I would genuinely love to know because it is a mystery to me. But if the rules are:

1) You have to agree with everything I say.

2) You have to love everything I wear.

3) You have to love everything I do.

4) You have to be insincere and tell me what I want to hear.

Then like the Dragons say on the TV show on Dragon's Den, I am sorry but I am out and the life of a hermit here I come.

The domestic goddess is a feminist

July 13, 2010

I am on the outrage bus at an outrageous article in The Daily Hate and a UK mum's online forum, are chipping in too, nodding furiously, and telling us to grab your pinny girls, keep the home fires burning and raise your children. Don't work, don't have a career; childrearing is a career, and this is where we really belong.

But it's black and white; have job and destroy your children's lives, or, be a housewife, nurture and cherish them and you won't ruin their lives. These are your only two options. I disagree; we could perhaps forge our own path, and take charge of our own destiny. We could create genuinely, flexible, working opportunities to enable us to retain some independence over our lives.

It has taken me a long time to find this path, but I have found a genuinely flexible working environment, which enables me to be there for my children and earn money. To be honest, I haven't even finished building my flexible empire. Retailer of the feminine and flowery home and fashion products, Cath Kidston, who exemplifies the domestic idealism to which we are all supposed to aspire, is clearly not a stay-at-home mum, but an entrepreneur who is building a financially strong business empire of her own!

Life doesn't stop when you have children. Yes, you juggle more and yes, you have to be flexible to ensure there is a balance between meeting their needs and your own needs. It is a choice, but it doesn't have to be one or the other. I would like to think that we are a community where we can help women balance both their intellectual needs and their domestic responsibilities. I love my children, and I love being with them, but they do not nourish me intellectually. As an independent, free thinking woman, I need more stimulation than the endless repetition of domesticity and the incarceration that being bound by this duty entails.

This challenge of how I balance my life is not as black and white as career vs. housewife. It is not one or the other. The world is a dynamic, evolving place and we are no longer bound by operating hours, within the constraints of 9 to 5, Monday to Friday. Do we need to adjust how we think, and only then can we achieve genuine liberation? Maybe the domestic goddess is a feminist; she outsources her housework, and mundane chores, raises her children, and runs her own business, so that she can have genuine flexibility?

The blissfully happy, stay-at-home mums lead a privileged existence because they can afford to stay-at-home, even with their alleged frugal living (pah! It's probably cheaper to holiday abroad than it is to holiday in delightful Kent and Scotland!). So are their faithful, employed husbands then not drinking, or swinging their fists, or withholding their housekeeping? These husbands happily give them direct access into the family coffers and they are handing over their pensions too, are they? What happens when he leaves her for a younger model, or they become another divorce statistic and are fighting for child support? Where does that leave the idealism of the homemaker? Women need to protect themselves and their children, because if you find yourself alone, without an income, and without a Prince Charming, then what?

The battle of the boobs and the bottle

July 25, 2010

Here is another ongoing battle of the bitches. Handbags ready, claws out! I have been thinking a lot recently about how us ladies are our own worst enemy.

Once again, we are trapped in battle where women challenge and question each other's choices, ultimately weakening our position, because we are fighting, instead of supporting, each other. In my experience, most women feel like they have been hit by a train when they have a baby. Nothing can prepare you for what is completely inconceivable in terms of pregnancy, birth and motherhood. You can read every book on the frickin' planet, you can have watched every one of your mates have kids, you may think you know what is coming, but the reality is 'bam! Incoming one (or more) baby, buckle up and brace yourself.'

At some point in the journey, the little parasites will trip you up and mess with your brain. If you are switched on, you'll realise that it's war! An ongoing battle for supremacy and it's either them, or you, as you spend the next few decades trying to regain control of your life again. And I say all this with a deep, unconditional, enduring love for my little demons. I can't tell you how many times I scream at The Grenade, 'do as you are told, you are not in charge!' and he screams back, 'why can't I be in charge?'

Sometimes we have long esoteric conversations about what he would do if he was in charge, but to cut it short, we would basically be living in the palace of childhood dreams, that is going to Toys R Us whenever he wanted and staying there for as long as possible.

Before we all get our knickers in a twist, bottle feeding is artificial but it is not fatal. I was solely bottle fed and I live to write this blog. There are many things about modern society which are artificial and unnaturally prolong life. If The Grenade and I had laboured together as nature intended we would both have died. He had the cord wrapped around his neck twice and under his arm. Both our vitals were fading as they ran down the corridor to give me an emergency C-section.

At the lowest point of the labour, if the doctor had said to me, 'now, you may die.' I would have replied, 'Thank you.' The Grenade was delivered artificially, with medical intervention, and we both survived because of it.

However, it is indisputable that giving babies breast milk is in their best interest. Breast milk is designed for them by the greatest architect in the world, Mother Nature. Being a parent is about sacrifice and I guess the challenge is managing the balance between sacrifice and martyrdom. Somehow, we have to be leaders, offer guidance, teach, grow, build our kids, while still coping with our own flawed existence.

We are all flawed. Nobody is perfect and we should stop fooling ourselves, if we think we are.

Seasonal work

July 29, 2010

Hagar called me from his office the other day because he was looking at the det plot (detachment plan to send folk into Afghanistan) and he was doing some logistical planning.

"Basically, I have got two options. I can either go for the whole summer, or Christmas and New Year," he said.

The summer is the fighting season. The insurgents (which fall loosely under the term Taliban, but are not all necessarily students of the cause, it's just an easy grouping to create the commonality of the enemy) are actually guns for hire that work seasonally. In the summer they fight the allied forces and in the winter they work in the poppy fields, harvesting the crop.

I used to work seasonally. I worked on the beaches of the Med in the summer and the slopes of the Alps in the winter. I worked for tour operators and would have to field banal guest questions such as;

"If I have porridge for breakfast, will I still be hungry at lunch time?"

"Will I be warm enough if I wear this jumper on top of the mountain?"

But the most regularly asked question was in the summer season;

"If you do this is in the summer, what do you do in the winter?"

In the end we used to make up answers to mix it up a bit.

"Oh, I am an Arctic seal clubber," I would reply.

Obviously, this is a very different type of seasonal work to your average Taliban insurgent.

Now, today, this summer is the fighting season, so while we enjoy our summer holidays, somewhere, in what feels likes another galaxy, the allied forces are battling to create stability in a wholly unstable environment. The allied forces are out in theatre, warring against the insurgents, as they fight hard for another big push in Helmand. The philosophy is clear; hold, build. Clear the ground of enemy, hold the ground, build a school or hospital, maybe mend a big fuck off dam (Kajaki). To governments and military leaders attrition is expected. The news of more death will trickle through daily.

They know in advance the loss of life is inevitable this summer. Maybe the people slurping their ice creams don't realise this as they shake their head and mourn with sadness as another casualty falls. It's the game of Risk but instead the stakes are higher and it's someone's son, or daughter, father or husband, wife or mother not an inanimate plastic figurine.

Decisions, decisions... For me, war aside for a minute, summer holidays means I'll take road trip with the kids for the whole summer and Christmas is such a family affair that I would rather he was with me, so I would choose the summer. But then, if you factor the war in then I would choose the winter because I would rather he was in the Afghanistan in the off season. Decisions, decisions...

In the end I said, "Hun, I don't mind. We'll work around you."

WARNING! Obnoxious and vulgar – like me!

August 3, 2010

First of all, I am going to apologise to Hagar's parents, who subscribe to the blog, because it's unlikely they have actually met this side of me. This post will be crass and vulgar, like me, when on the whole I tend to curb my more potty mouth and fast talking obnoxiousness when I am around them. I am also going to apologise to the lovely, kind, nice people, who may have an inkling that I have the subtlety of a bull in a china shop, but that I have actually been sort of repressing it until now. If you don't like swearing, bums, poo, bottom burps and a crass sense of humour then please stop, and go and do something far more worthwhile than reading the rest of this post.

Last night I read this blog called Pajamas and Coffee and I realised that I was suppressing myself a little in my blog's postings. Pajamas and Coffee is a fabulously unashamed, energetic, bouncy, brilliant blog full of honesty and I thought it was great. Plus I am feeling a bit glum today due to insomnia issues that I have, because I suffer from 'busy head'. Once that little puppy kicks into action then there is no stopping it and I am up through the night thinkity thunking in a tiggerific kind of way.

Frankly, it's tiring and annoying and the only cure is a couple of episodes of 'Two and Half Men' which seems to send me to the land of sleepy nods. Anyway, I need to cheer myself up and hopefully spread some of the laughter around about it.

The thing is that I have a puerile, immature sense of humour. I can't help it. I am Finbarr Saunders from Viz. I think farting is funny. I love a good knob gag (and I am not talking about deep throat 'snigger, snigger'). I never fail to crack a smile when I get a notification from Skype saying that 'Rob came online'. Even yesterday, I received a reply to a comment I had made on Single Parent Dad's post about baby gravy and he replied by saying; 'I come with a horrendous disclaimer' and I thought immediately; 'most men cum with a bit of a grunt.'

My two favourite jokes are:

How do you get a nun pregnant?

Fuck her

OR

What's the difference between oral sex and anal sex?

Oral sex makes your day but anal sex makes your hole weak.

Not because I think that it's funny that anal sex weakens your botty cavity but just because I like that it's a clever play on words. (I am also not advocating nun fucking, nuns have a right to be celibate).

I like the one where the man says to his mate, 'what would you do if a bird shits on your head?'

'Well, I wouldn't go out with her again,' his mate replies.

I like the play on words. It amuses me in a childish way.

Also, I get bored really easily, and when I get bored I get mischievous. I think it's funny to do things without really thinking of the possible consequences. For example, there was a Facebook application called 'Interview Questions'. One of my friends suggested I get said app, which I dutifully did. But I didn't really know how Facebook worked, so I thought I was answering the questions simply for her amusement. The questions were fairly pedestrian, and so, for a cheap laugh, I decided I would spice it up a bit.

One of the questions was:

What is your favourite body part?

(Snigger, snigger) I thought that I would be very clever and write something rude that I thought was very funny! About 10 minutes later my friend calls me and says, 'what have you just written?'

On her news feed for all her friends, and also my friends to see, Facebook had streamed:

A Modern Military Mother has just answered 'I am quite partial to hard cock' to an Interview question. To find out more about her click here!'

Whoops! I am not really a very yummy mummy, I don't ice cupcakes and I don't own any Cath Kidston stuff. This is me - I drink too much, I eat too much, I swear too much. I am outstandingly average, utterly flawed and unashamedly happy to be so. Welcome to my blog.

A family affair

August 11, 2010

A truly splendid day! RAF Odiham Families Day was spectacular. My feet hurt but I have that warm, buzzy feeling that you get after a thoroughly splendiferous time. The ethos behind any Families Day is a chance for the military to say thank you to the families, without whose enduring support and sacrifice the work of those who serve would not be possible.

The highlight was, of course, The Grenade's and my 20-minute jaunt over Basingstoke, in the magnificent MkIII CH47, AKA the Chinook helicopter. I was so excited as we arrived at the station. Unpacking the car, I could hear the ambient thud of the rotors in the distance. As we walked up to the airfield, the marvellous sight of four parked aircraft greeted us with their blades turning. These are the same workhorses that are used tirelessly to support UK training operations and UK based tasking.

The Grenade and I left Hagar with The Menace, and Mrs Vino, The Little Moo and Game Boy (our guests for the day) while we queued for our helicopter adventure. We were ushered into the main briefing room and took our seats.

After about 20 minutes, we were shown a short Health & Safety briefing video.

When it had finished the Flight Lieutenant, who was giving the brief said, "Simple enough. Any questions? Any questions?"

'Shit.' I thought, 'what's he going to say?' He can be very unpredictable. I was checking the exits to see how I could surreptitiously leave without drawing any further attention to ourselves.

"Yes, young man," said the young officer.

'Damn!' I thought.

"I am SO going to get airborne!" he gleefully declared.

"Yes, you are. Good question," came the reply.

A huge sense of relief swept over me as we shuffled out of the room to our next queue. Unsurprisingly, the whole thing had been organised with military precision. There were four tents, one for each aircraft. We were allocated to aircraft 4, and were on the second trip of the day. As we were waiting, the first trip was coming in to land.

Inside the holding tent, before embarkation, we were given our helmets.

The beauty of the helmet was that it muffled out all the noise of the rumbling rotors, and also, the wittering of The Grenade, who was asking me a barrage of questions that I couldn't answer.

"When we go up in the aircraft mummy will we not be able to breathe because the air is thinner?" He said.

"No, we won't be going up that high."

"How high will we be going?"

"Probably beneath the clouds."

"But will we go above the clouds, and then the air will get thinner."

"No! We are not going above the clouds."

"Is the air thinner below the clouds?"

"No."

"Why not?"

'AAAAARGGHHHH!' Silent screaming.

"I know, why don't you ask Daddy these questions, when we get off?" I politely, patiently and calmly suggested. Science was never my one of my strong subjects. Why does he never ask me one on art and literature, or about the plot in Grey's Anatomy, or why women should be cherished?

A bit more waiting and then it was time to get onboard. The Grenade was really excited, but also really cautious. He clung to my arm tightly and weighed it down like a lead weight. As we walked across the dispersal, the noise of the blades thundering round reverberated through my body. Each step brought us closer to the roaring beast, until, as we neared the ramp, we were blasted by hot flushes of air, blown out by the enormous exhausts either side of the cabin.

Directed by the crewman, all rigged up in their helmets and flying suits with winding leads and cable adorning them, we walked up the ramp, took our seats and tightly fastened our seat belts. Once everyone was strapped in, the Chinook lifted like a big rumbling wobble board. I felt a surge in my stomach. The air was thick and cushioned. I felt sick. The helicopter lunged upwards and the pilot rolled it to the right. We were airborne at last.

The Grenade beamed and was silent. He was silenced with awe at the magic of flight.

I love the colour palette of the Chinook's interior. The contrast of the bright redness of the straps against the hard seats, and the shiny, and yet dull, grey stitched diamond check of the interior.

For 20 minutes, we rumbled, rattled and rolled. I mainly felt sick. I wished I hadn't skipped breakfast. Note to self; don't fly in Chinook on empty stomach.

Very soon it was over. We rattled back to base with a big final lunge on the way down.

Then we disembarked, down the ramp and across the dispersal, back to the tent to hand the helmets back.

Seamlessly executed and exhilarating. It was great. A real treat and something for which we are truly grateful. Thank you so much RAF Odiham.

The Grenade and I joined a very disgruntled Hagar.

"Awright love?" I said.

"SHEeee has been a complete nightmare." (By SHEeee he means The Menace). "I can't take my eyes off her for a second, otherwise she is off, and so I have to chase after her. This happens all the time!"

'Hmmm' I think to myself, 'sounds fairly par for the course to me.'

"That's not a nightmare, that's normal," I said.

"But it's really stressful and annoying," he bleated.

"Honey - it's called parenting!" I said, shaking my head in despair.

The rest of the day involves a balancing act between keeping everybody happy, children and adults alike and there is so much to do that it isn't a problem. There's free standing aircraft, fairground rides, lots of display stands, an arsenal of military stuff, plus the Mother's Union are giving out tea, coffee and free cakey buns. Above, there's an air display that lasts for the whole afternoon. The kids run riot. We scatter, come back together, catch up with old friends, scatter, and come back together again endlessly, all day.

We were waiting for the RAF Falcons to jump out of Chinook, at a height where the air was probably a snipsy bit thinner, when I felt The Menace tugging at my trousers.

"Ass cream, mama" she said, as she looked lovingly at me with her baby blues.

'Ay?' I thought. 'Surely she's too young for haemorrhoids, and anyway, how would she know?'

"Ass cream, mama," and points at a little boy eating a Mr Whippy 99.

"Oh!" The penny drops. "You want an ice cream bubba."

Men and war

August 18, 2010

I have been thinking a lot about feminism and equality nowadays partly because despite my innate sense of I can do whatever the fuck I want regardless of my gender, I somehow have ended up a married, subjugated, incarcerated, unpaid slave to my children and husband. Oh yes, and I earn money too. How the fuck did that happen? The conclusion that I have come to is that the journey for equality is an impossible destination. Men and women are not equal just like salt and pepper are not equal. How do you make salt and pepper equal? You can't - it's impossible. Men and women can never be equal because we are completely different.

Before I get sucked into a debate of outraged hens clucking about equality - I am not saying that we give up the fight girls - I am just saying we need to change our tactics and play a different game. Salt and pepper, yin and yang, black and white - diametrically opposed differences between men and women have never been so heavily illustrated as in the film Restrepo, the documentary that accompanies Sebastian Junger's book, War. Blogger, London City Mum and I had our first date, popcorn free, in a private cinema in Soho House. The film is brilliant and compelling viewing, but it's not for the faint-hearted. It's like watching the TV series, Band of Brothers, or Pacific, but it's not a drama with actors – it's real. People really die. It's raw and honest. But I sat in the cinema saddened by the impossible war. Like salt and pepper, like men and women, the Taliban and the US soldiers are diametrically opposed and they will never find a solution, not in this decade. The only common ground is that both sides are fighting men, and men need war.

I watched this film and I thought men really do need war. War is about the size of your penis. It is the ultimate knob battle. Men create weapons that are an extension of their penis and discharging these weapons is about hosing the planet with an explosively packed charge of destructive semen. The bigger the weapon, the bigger the penis, the more intensive the explosion, the more intensively they shoot their load. War and fighting is about men, hard-ons and ejaculation. They are programmed to hunt, kill and protect their territory. But the men are out of control because the universe is out of balance.

Is America imperialist? "If you help me, I will make you rich," said the Major to the Taliban elder. If this was Star Wars, the

Taliban would be the rebel alliance and the allied forces would be the Empire. I have never shot a real gun, but I am interested to know what it feels like because I can imagine it's very empowering. Are there any weapons that can't be a penis and ejaculation metaphor? By this I mean that discharging a weapon is like male ejaculation. I don't know enough about warfare and weapons to say this conclusively, but this is what my instincts are saying.

Men like fighting and they like blowing shit up. They are united as a gender and they are in charge. Women fight with each other and let men get away with all sorts of unacceptable behaviour. We are not united. If women really united would we be able to stop war happening? It's a pretty massive ask, isn't it? But someone has to cuff those men folk around the ear and put them on the naughty step. Let's face it, you wouldn't let your husband and son masturbate in the living room would you? But it's all right for them to go discharging their weapons when someone takes their lolly, is it?

Fear of Flying and
Dawn French

September 10, 2010

I am just going to ease you in. Things will start more hectically next week. I am chilled because I have been reading, in between the children and Hagar driving me nuts, and lying naked on the sun bed. It's not a pretty sight; but liberating and lovely to do.

We have just spent two weeks at our fab house in the Limousin.

I quickly devoured Dear Fatty by Dawn French. It's an easy read. She is definitely a heroine of mine. But I felt weirdly connected to her for many reasons. In the end I wrote this email to her agent, in the style of her tome and I said:

Dear Ms Dawn French, Impresario of Magnificent Humour, chocolate and Inter-Galactic Divine Feminine Goddess of Greatness,

Please help me. I am your mother. Well, O.K. not exactly your actually birth mother, but more a modern incarnation of her. What I am trying to say is this – I am the wife of an RAF pilot (Hagar the horrible) and I have two kids, a boy

(The Grenade, aged 7) and a girl (The Menace, aged 2). As well as being a wife and mother, I am a writer of a blog called:

http://amodernmilitarymother.com

This blog is tales from the domestic frontline and I write it for all women that are married to the MOD and find themselves frequently married, single, celibate.

I would lurve you to please read my blog and see if you like it. If you like it, I would love you to become an unpaid, altruistic, kind ambassador for my blog and endorse it saying things like:

"This blog is dead good. You should read it because it says stuff that is important and also sometimes it's funny."

If you do then I will buy you one of them new white chocolate oranges.

Just by the by, here are some tenuous reasons why you and me is weirdly connected:

- I went to Uni in Plymouth so I know what a Janner is - I grew up in Warminster which is near where you and Mr Henry lived when you was betrothed - I was born in York, which is where Terry's make their chocolate oranges - My mum committed suicide.

Please help me for so many reasons but mainly because you can and I need some help. But also because I have always thought you were amazing, since the days of The Tube and I have grown up loving your work, plus you seem nice. You seem like the sort of person, who isn't too famous to help someone like me, if you felt what I was doing was worth it, which I think it is, clearly.

Lots of love, AMMM

Dear Fatty, is all about Dawn French's life written as a series of letters to her dearly beloved friends. Her father was in the RAF and she had an older brother. It's warm, funny, engaging and in places deeply tragic. Just like life really. At the end of it I wanted to be one of Dawn French's friends because she seems lovely. I think it could be known as a girl crush.

Mary Mac, at Pajamas and Coffee, recommended Fear of Flying by Erica Jong in her blog. In the 70's it was seen as the epitome of sexual liberation and female emancipation. Isadora, the main protagonist, unhappy in her second marriage, is dreaming of the zipless fuck. It's a poignant read for me, but not because of sexual emancipation, but because it made me realise that I am not honest in my writing. I am giving you my best side. I am not telling you about my fat tummy, my stretch marks, my varicose veins, the ugly things I have done in my life, the things I regret, the people I have hurt and my certain intolerances. I am also not telling you about my true naughtiness and liberation, my genuine freedoms, my soaring mind that is limitless in my thoughts of infinite possibilities. I am not sure if I am really ready to let you know what a twat I can be and those moments that make my toes curl up to the sky. I am not sure if many people in my life are ready for my honesty and absolute truth; so for now I will just tell you about one truth. This is the story of one of my zipless fucks because to be truthful there have been a few.

According the Urban Dictionary, it can be defined as thus: "A phrase coined by Erica Jong in the book 'Fear of Flying'. As described by her – It is a sexual encounter between strangers that has the swift compression of a dream and is seemingly free of all remorse and guilt. It is absolutely pure, there is no power game and it is free of ulterior motives. It has also been described as the perfect one night stand.

"The zipless fuck is the purest thing there is, rarer than the unicorn and I have never had one." – Fear of Flying

It was only after reading the Fear of Flying that I understood that I had in fact already experienced the zipless fuck and that it had happened some 15 years ago before I knew that I was feminist. I have always thought I was free and I always have exercised my freedoms without guilt. Even today I don't feel guilty that I am incarcerated by marriage and children. I just feel trapped like a caged bear looking for the key and working out how to unlock the door and release myself. So this zipless fuck happened when I was a student, at The College of St Mark and St John, or Marjons as it was known.

I was in my third year, and one day on campus I spied a fine looking specimen. He was young, handsome, lean and trendy, like a young David Beckham before tattoos; not quite Michelangelo's David – he wasn't perfection - but he was beautiful, sculptured, young, dumb and full of cum.

But I could see inside his soul and it was clear that he had no depth. (Yes, I judged him and he was probably a young incarnation of Freud, but that is highly unlikely as most students at Marjons were studying to be PE teachers and I believe him to be one of those, so not that sharpest tool in the tin – no offence meant). He was what I would define as a man 'who is just for Christmas and not for life'. All of the best zipless fucks I have had are mute – the men don't speak. I can't engage in dialogue with them as it ruins the perfection. During my first bodged zipless fuck I did try conversation, but it just revealed how wholly incompatible we were really were.

"Ssh, sssh, ssh!" No speaking; just primitive, carnal, mutual consenting, protected fucking please.

Thursday night was JFK's student night and it was dominated by Marjons. Later on in the night, I was leaning across the bar ordering cheap poison when the specimen stood next to me looking as hot as ever. In my drunkenness and without a care in the world, I leaned across and said; "How about you and me go back to my place for a no strings attached fuck?"

He looked at me and without hesitation he said, "O.K."

So we left the club, jumped in a taxi and headed back to my shared house.

What ensued was a night of animal passion and rampant humping. Safe sex, of course, welly boots and wetsuits. It was a great night, which resulted in carpet burns on my shoulders.

In the morning we both woke up and I looked across him and said; "And your name is?"

He said, "Didn't we do this last night?"

"Just refresh my memory."

He did reply, but I still can't remember his name. All I can remember is that he was a deckchair attendant from Bridlington. There you have one of my zipless fucks. The perfect one night stand. I didn't care that I didn't see him again and I didn't want to see him again. He felt the same. We had agreed it from the start. All I wanted from him was that one great night. I don't regret it one bit. He was hotter than a snake's ass and I even thought that in the morning. Is this the act of true emancipation? Or do you think I am a floozy? I don't consider this to be the act of a floozy because I was single and I assume he was single, although I didn't ask as it would have ruined the moment – I wasn't interested in exploring his personality. We were both consenting and we were sexually responsible, irresponsibly together. This is the freedom of the emancipated women, to make these choices and to live with the consequences without judgement.

In the Fear of Flying Erica Jong's main protagonist is still in a Cinderella fairytale narrative – men hold the answer to a woman's happiness. She is still seeking their protection and permission to be loved. True emancipation is that the secret to happiness is found within ourselves and not from others. I am looking for the balance between men and women so that we are equally appreciated for our contribution and we are not slaves to each other.

Do women watch war films?

October 8, 2010

Tim Hetherington and Sebastian Junger were embedded for 10 months with the US Army; but I feel like I have been embedded with the RAF for the last 10 years. An anthropological observer, trying to understand and navigate the plethora of unwritten codes of conduct and expectation. Up until last year, when Hagar was deployed, I would bury my head in the sand, crack open the wine, count up to the middle and down again until he came home, whilst avoiding the news as much as possible. I didn't even want to look at the war. In the 12 years we have been together he has been to Northern Ireland, Sierra Leone, Bosnia, Iraq (approx 4 times) and Afghanistan (approx 4 times) – although, to be honest, I lose count. I would say that probably over 50% of our relationship has been apart. At one point, he was doing 8 weeks on and 8 weeks off, so 'going to war' just became part of our everyday life.

The tempo of ops for all the Chinook guys and gals is high. In fact, Hagar was awarded a Mention-In-Despatches after one deployment for some daring do. It was difficult to know what to say, how to support him because his 'away journey' was one I could never understand. There wasn't a break for either of us. It's hard to explain it, but this bouncing apart and coming together, with profound life-changing experiences happening in an unknown country, with ramifications, and meanings, that aren't everyday dinner conversations, are hard to put into words, and so, often, he didn't. He just brooded, and found his own way back to us, whilst I watched and waited in the eaves of his darkness, for the unravelling to occur.

In September 2008, I began researching, and writing, a battlefield memoir about the role of the Chinooks, in Afghanistan, and in the British Armed Forces. Suddenly, I was forced to confront face-on a subject matter that I had been purposefully ignoring. I was very lucky to be surrounded by experts that helped and supported me on my journey; starting at The Great Game, to the fall of the Northern Alliance, to September 11th, to the Bonn Agreement. I had always buffered my fears with the certain comfort that the Chinook is the best defended aircraft, and the aviation best bet, for my own warrior-class serviceman.

The whole tempo of the memoir was centred around the notion that the Taliban had identified the CH47 (Chinook) as a glory target. They called it the cow. It was the ultimate prize to down one, and dance around it, showcasing their majesty to the world.

Never in the history of the British Chinook force had an aircraft been shot down in combat.

I laid down the 100,000 word manuscript in 10 weeks in an intensive, marathon writing session, where I became unnaturally immersed in a conflict I had never visited, flying an aircraft I had never flown, as a person I would never be. One month after the book hit the bookshelves, the worst happened. Hagar got a call at midnight, summoning him to work. I knew before the story broke in the media. A British Chinook had been shot down in Afghanistan. The first ever in its history. I knew the pilot. I knew the pilot that picked them up. It felt up, close and very personal, and I had a hugely disproportionate reaction to it and freaked out. This cushion of safety, of vigilance, of aircraft redundancy, of training and being the best they could be, shattered around me and all over of a sudden I was hit with the undeniable reality of the true danger of Afghanistan. A danger that I had been blissfully, and ignorantly, ignoring as a coping mechanism for the endless churn of ops that I was enduring from the domestic frontline.

Since the book was published, I bravely look the 'war machine' in the eye and try to make sense of the conflict. All the research and understanding hasn't made me any wiser. I am just frustrated by the complexity of the problem. I am a problem solver. I am a fixer and Afghanistan is an intricate, layered, very tricky puzzle indeed.

So as a wife of a serviceman do I watch war films? The answer is yes, I do. I have done since before I met Hagar. The first war film I loved was 'Sink the Bismarck'.

Hagar and I watched Band of Brothers and Pacific religiously. They are brilliant depictions of combat. In fact, I think Restrepo is the documentary that Band of Brothers would have been if it had been recorded in real time; in the same way Tim and Sebastian recorded Restrepo. The notion of brotherhood at the heart of the war machine that I discussed with Tim when I interviewed him, is not new but it has never been so acutely and accurately captured as in the making of Restrepo.

The wives and families of Restrepo troops watched the film, and gleaned an understanding of what their loved ones had experienced at the outpost. One wife said; "I wish I had seen Restrepo before my divorce, it'd given me an understanding of my ex-husband's experience that I wish I had had while I was with him. He never shared."

When I spoke with Major Dan Kearney, who was the senior officer of the platoon followed in the documentary Restrepo, he told me he had stopped feeling. He had buried his emotions, deep inside his soul and thrown away the key. Men are not sharers. Sharing is a sign of weakness. The men of Restrepo are warriors;

they are Spartans. They write tattoos shouting "Stop Feeling Sorry For Yourself". The military men want you to understand by osmosis what they have experienced, and then instinctively know how to empathise, love and support them as they internalise their pain and emotions. At the sharp end of combat, tattooed in war paint, armed and braced for battle the young Spartan is an adrenaline charged, fighting, macho machine. But in the aftermath, in the comedown of combat, in the bosom of home, when the adrenaline surges out of his body; he is a boy again, with skin, bones, and feelings that he would rather not have.

As a wife of a military pilot and the mother of a young son, there is a lot to be gained from watching Restrepo. It's a brave watch, with a window into battle. It shows that "war is not the glorious adventure depicted on films; it's cruel, destructive and worst of all, indiscriminate in the slaughter and maiming of women and children and non-combatants who play no part in the conflict" (source unknown).

But it is a film of great energy and spirit. It will take you into the soul of the soldier and help you understand the highs and lows, the strength and the vulnerabilities, and the intensity of war. Sometimes, you need to look at things you don't want to see to understand the things you can't see.

What's interesting for me is that two very serious, ageing social observers and recorders, Sebastian Junger and Tim Hetherington, went into the edge of Armageddon and got so much more then they had ever bargained for. They became ensconced; enchanted by the brotherhood and joined them. I suspect that was not what they foresaw at all.

At the launch of Infidel, Tim Hetherington's last book, he stood before the room and he looked exposed and vulnerable like a Ninja Turtle without his shell. But, I can imagine embedded in battle, with his flak jacket and camera, shooting his own weapon, he is in a warrior-class of his own.

The creation of his book, the film Restrepo, and Sebastian Junger's book War, have a created an incredible insight to the psyche of the soldier. Infidel, the leather bound, black, stunning, book of creativity is a homage to the Spartan Warrior, from the outpost Restrepo.

A collection of moving, beautiful, tragic and uplifting images, recording and illustrating the feral, adrenaline charged pack of brothers that fought on the edge of a mountain, trying to build a road, fighting an enemy they couldn't see and didn't really understand, but knew hated them; the Infidel.

Operation bangers & mash

October 25, 2010

Hagar has been back less than 24 hours and we have already had our first fight. This is not unusual so please don't be alarmed. It's part of the re-integration and also in establishing, who has worked the hardest and is the most tired. (Ahem! Obviously, it's me!)

I have had a fairly full-on 10 days. The Menace has taken her destruction to new levels of patience testing. Her latest occupation is to wait until I am engaged in a domestic chore elsewhere, take the stool from the under counter to the work surface, climb onto the work surface and then create some form of havoc. Things like drop jelly sweets into the toaster, eat all the biscuits or her latest pastime of scooping washing powder out of the box and spreading it liberally around the kitchen.

This coupled with hunt the poo, as she is nearly ready to be potty trained and so is randomly curling them down, is enough to send me nuts. Washing powder is a tricky clean because you have to keep it dry to clean it efficiently. It's fair to say that I am knackered, plus I am an insomniac and a snipsy bit manic.

When Hagar returns from 'away' the two worlds don't necessarily collide harmoniously. Although, I did manage to stay on top of the domestic chores, the powder incidents (x3) and an accidental unexpected alcoholic excess meant that I was a little bit behind on my admin. Being the doting wife I had shopped for a roastie dinner but neglected to take the joint out of the freezer early enough so by 4pm, it was fairly obvious that Roast Pork was off the menu. I was fairly certain that I had some sausages in the freezer and that we would be able to re-adjust the supper menu to bangers & mash instead. Hagar and I agreed that we would eat at 6.30pm.

He then asked me to get the sausages out of the freezer. To be honest, this is where our stories begin to conflict. He seems to think that I had agreed to this request. I am fairly certain that I just ignored him and mostly likely thought 'get the sausages yourself.' It's highly possible I didn't articulate this thought and just carried on doing what I was doing.

At around 5 p.m. Hagar asked me if I had got the sausages out of the freezer. I replied that I hadn't. He then stomped into the garage to get them himself, only to discover much to his chagrin that I had in fact mis-informed him about how well stocked the freezer was in the sausage department and there weren't enough sausages in the freezer after all.

Enraged by this complete communication failure on my part, he then draws the conclusion that he is in fact going to have to drive to the supermarket and purchase some sausages if we are to have the agreed bangers & mash. He is clearly very disgruntled about this and very grumpily drove to Tesco and bought some sausages for tea.

On his return I then have the audacity to suggest that he could do with perhaps 'chilling out' over the lack of sausages and I even very generously acknowledged that I was in fact 'wrong' about the quantity of sausages in the freezer. On further discussion, we discovered that Hagar had just returned from a fairly stressful exercise, where they had achieved in a very condensed period what they had originally intended to do in a longer period of time. I won't bore you with details. It was during this rather intense explanation that I began to chuckle and then giggle, with a bit of snorting. Hagar was explaining to me that if he wanted something done at work he would task the very young and thrusting officers on his squadron to do something, then they would expedite it immediately and with knobs on. He, too then finally cracked a smile.

It was becoming very clear to me that I had clearly failed on Operation Bangers & Mash (er...bovvered).

If Hagar had been at work and said to one of these young officers, 'go and get the sausages from the freezer', the officer in question would have gone to the freezer established that we were out of sausages, then got in his car gone to the supermarket, and if they didn't have any sausages he would have gone to the pig farm, slaughtered a pig and made him some sausages because that is the kind of energetic and enthusiastic young men that he has on his flight. Therefore, to come home and issue an instruction and to just quite frankly be ignored was not what he was used too. Hey hum, he's home now and I am glad that we managed to get that first row squared away early. It's broken the ice and I have managed to re-establish the standard operating procedures of chaos and insolence. Operation Bangers & Mash was not the best executed of military exercises but I did manage to get the supper on the table TOT (time on target) 18:30 despite my complete insubordination and terrible intelligence on sausages stocks in the freezer.

The cost of a wife

December 15, 2010

If I died Hagar couldn't deploy. He would have to stop flying. We have two kids. He would be responsible for them. My mum died in 1974. I was 2 years old. My dad hadn't insured her. He had insured himself to the hilt in case of his own death so that she wouldn't go without but he had under-valued the impact of her role in the advent of her death. We have talked about this since. It wasn't a malicious act. Maybe it was a reflection of the attitude at the time.

Her death was unexpected. It was sudden and tragic. He was left solely in charge of me. He had to sacrifice his blossoming career to raise me. He was working as a British Rail manager doing some type of operations role at the rail freight terminal in Anglesey, Holyhead. Not far from RAF Valley and not far from where Kate & Wills will be setting up home. (I hope she has more fun there then my mother did!) For a few years he was a single parent.

Not so long ago, I was having a cuppa with a milly wife, whose husband had deployed for six months, and she said to me something along the lines of, 'my other half doesn't mind if I don't work because it would cost £24,000 in childcare if I wasn't around.'

I nearly choked on my brew! And the rest! It was then I started thinking about the cost of my replacement in the advent of my death, or severe disabling, (divorce doesn't count) in order for Hagar to deploy for 6 months of the year, plus attend the exercises and also do the night flying, to deliver his life to the same standard that he experiences right now, he would require at least:

3 x full time qualified nannies (£30k p.a each), 1 x housekeeper (£275 per week – £13k p.a), 1 x part-time gardener (£2000k p.a), 1 x part-time personal assistant (£100 per week – £4800 p.a)

Approx £109,000 p.a – which is considerably more than he earns.

We don't have the family back up that could step in and help either just in case you were thinking he could palm the kids off to his mother or mine. Mine is dead. His is too old to handle our two kids even now when we are both alive!

In reality, he couldn't even afford to hire me at my commercial rates as a freelance consultant. I make an expensive cup of tea.

But the hard facts are that, even though I am insured, if I was to die Hagar would have to give up flying and could no longer deploy.

The taxpayer has invested well over £3 million pounds to keep Hagar operational and current so that he can deliver his role at the sharpest end of the pointiest bit of the conflict. Once you are father you have responsibilities to your children that are solely yours and the mother of your children's. It shouldn't be under-estimated, the value of the role the supporting parent gives to the service, to enable the serving parents to deploy and fight for their country. I can only say what I see in my own home but Hagar loves his job. He wants to deploy and he wants to serve his country. It's not for me to stop him and I support him without complaining (I truly do!). But honestly, I do think the partners are paid lip service to, that we are an embuggerance that has to be tolerated and the role we give is not wholly appreciated, or the enormity of it is taken for granted.

Hagar doesn't even see half the stuff that gets done in our house. In fact, he once made the mistake of arguing that he did 50% of the domestic chores. 'Interesting!' I thought.

'I know' I said, 'I have an idea. You write down a list of all the jobs that need to be done and then put a percentage next to it indicating how the jobs are divvied up.'

Hagar was feeling pretty bullish at this point. He was fairly confident that he was going to prove his point and the status quo that he was aiming for would return.

But alas, it was not to be so because the reality was when he formed the list and allocated his percentages to all the tasks that we have as a family unit, he omitted at least 50% of the jobs from the list, because he didn't even know that those jobs were being done in the first place!

Would the tax payer be willing to bear the cost so the widowed father can deploy and they can get their return on investment? Err... No! They would recommend his children were fostered instead. But it's a crying shame that a woman has to die before her true value is appreciated.

I guess like Joni Mitchell sang in Big Yellow Taxi, 'Don't it always seem to go that you don't know what you've got 'til it's gone.' My Christmas wish is this; I wish that the world would stop taking women for granted. NB: Turkeys don't vote for Christmas so very few men are going to say 'I agree. Yes, let me do more!' And the battle continues...

Waiting for change

January 9, 2011

21st September 1997 was the day that I learned that I had no control over my life. It was the start of the Whitbread Round the World Race and I had blagged my way onto an 8 metre RIB (rigid inflatable boat) with a 350HP inboard engine so that I could watch the start.

I had drafted a book proposal to follow and document the team Silk Cut, called Silk Cut: Uncut, which was about to be submitted to publishers by my agent. I was dreaming of trotting the globe, observing and recording the debauchery of promiscuous and carefree, hardcore ocean racers. I felt like I had my whole life ahead of me and it was a life of adventure and travel; my most favourite things in the entire universe.

The start was majestic. I never tire of watching powerful ocean racing yachts charge away into the sun. The Farr 60 ocean-going beasts of that generation of racing were the first of a new class of offshore ocean racing yachts that could reach top speeds of 30 knots.

They were lighter, enduring and performed better. There was a frisson of tension amongst the skippers, as they feared the beast and didn't know what could be unleashed traversing the oceans over long distances with all this power and strength at their fingertips. Yet, although they feared for their lives, at the same time like racehorses pounding at the gate, they couldn't wait to put them through their paces.

The fleet of spectator boats turned the tidal waters of the Solent into a torrential washing machine of lines and rivers of bubbling cold, salty, white foam. We were in the best boat to watch a start. A powerful, rumbling monster of a RIB with the thrust and dexterity required to weave in and out of the fleet. We matched the speeds of the yachts as they battled for the lead, to display their mettle amongst the crowded waters, to glean a moral victory, to lead the charge out into the ocean, to gain the competitive advantage and to keep us guessing about how the race would play out. It was exhilarating to be a part of. The September sun beamed gloriously all day and I felt completely alive as the cool, salty air swirled around me.

Once we watched the boats sail into the distance at the Needles, we turned around and headed home. We were one of the last spectator boats to turn. Many had not pushed as far up as we had. The water was flat now; a glassy mill-pond.

The RIB bounced and flew deftly across the sea, like a pebble skimming the waves. We were all still buzzing. I was standing at the front holding onto the bow painter (the rope from the front). The rope was taut; I was leaning back and absorbing the wave impact by bending my knees (just like you do when you ski over mogul hills). I was used to boats. I had been driving RIBs professionally for 5 years.

The driver started to mess around for a laugh. The sea around us was calm and I was holding my own on the painter. Then out of nowhere a long, slow, wake of a ferry rippled across our path. The driver didn't see it, and I didn't see it. It acted as ramp for the RIB, which was travelling at 20 knots and the boat took off. As I was holding onto to the taut painter it acted like a pendulum, I took off too. It lifted me a foot off the ground. As the boat landed on the hardened water surface, I landed on the floor of the RIB. As I landed my ankle twisted and I landed on it. I felt it snap. There was initially no pain. 'Shit! I have broken my ankle.' I said. 'I have to elevate it.'

With that I lay down on the deck and raised my leg onto the port sponson (left side inflatable tube). I had indeed broken my ankle. I had clean snapped my tibia and fibula. I ended up having re-constructive surgery that lasted 5 hours with 11 titanium pins and a metal plate.

I hadn't planned to break my leg. I wasn't ready for it to happen.

I learnt that day that I have no control over my life and so stopped planning my future from that day forth.

On the 28th December 2010 Hagar was arrested and charged with sexual assault. Another wave I didn't see coming. The universe had sent me to Dubai. I was coming here anyway for a rest, which I needed desperately, but now I feel like I have been sent here to wait for change. I know that change is coming. The transition has already started. In the meantime, I am here in Dubai, reflecting in the glorious sunshine, pondering a future I can't control and wondering how it's going to play out.

I'm a feminist not a lesbian

June 21, 2011

Last week, I was invited to speak at Farnborough Ladies Night because one of the organisers had seen an article by the Fleet Courier that the book I co-wrote, Immediate Response, had been a given a medal by The Military Writers Society of America. I am not sure what the ladies were expecting but I think it was something a little more twee than me. Perhaps they were expecting a demure, domestic goddess, who would proudly regale them with tales of awe inspiring derring-do and keeping the homes fire burning. Instead, they were presented with my candid analysis of how I constantly battle with my husband to pull his weight more in the house.

My opening line was; "I am a feminist not a lesbian." The ladies, whose ages ranged from 50 to 80 years old, engaged immediately. I could see them lift their droopy lids and either bristle or giggle. I had two camps – those that looked at me with complete disgust and those who chuckled in naughty delight.

The challenge that I often face, when I proudly out myself as a card-carrying feminazi, is defining what I mean. Especially because the common conception of feminism is that you are a bean-eating, carpet-munching communist. (No offence intended to those of feminist lesbian communist vegetarian persuasion – it's just that I am not that way inclined). Hence my opening gambit.

It's tough because I haven't created an academic thesis to qualify this bold and brash declaration. But what I truly seek is freedom. Freedom to do what I want when I want. Genuine independence. This I don't have through my own misguided choices. Shall I tell you who I blame? To quote the popular film, Pretty Woman – "Cinder-fucking-rella". I walked into the Cinderella honey trap and stupidly fell in love, got married and had children. Doh! Bam! I sold my independence down the river.

I feel like recently I have had an epiphany. I want my freedom back. I want my independence. I want to do what I want, when I want. Mission on. The reason why it is a mission is because obviously there are people in my life and they are part of what I want. I don't mean that I want to run away and abandon my choice, that is not what I want. It's about finding the right balance between my own needs and those to whom I am responsible.

I think I gave up my freedom too easily. It was easier to take on the burden of responsibility and do-it-myself. In fact, I closed my talk to the Farnborough ladies with some observations on my 8 year old son, The Grenade. I said that I was just going to have to apologise to all his girlfriends because his will to do what he wants is often greater than mine to prevent him behaving in a burping, farting, slobbing gregariously male way. The note would read; 'I am sorry. I did my best. Please don't hold it against me. Honestly, it's not my fault.'

Clearly, in my younger years I blamed my mother-in-law for ruining Hagar and turning him into the flawed man that walks alongside the other flawed men in the species. However, now I am a mother to a son I realise that I have been very disloyal to his mother. It's not her fault. I was blaming the wrong parent – it was his dad's fault! Mwah ha ha! I am only joking. It's not their fault really.

So my mission is on. Wish me luck. Thank you Farnborough ladies for what was a very entertaining evening. It was great to share and learn that the trials and tribulations that I face, you too have a faced and, although there have been changes, the majority of women face that are still slaves to domesticity.

I think I am back in the blogosphere – I have missed it so much. Blogging gives me a great sense of freedom. It's my blog and I can write what I want to. I am back.

Hagar Goes To Afghanistan

July 2, 2011

Has Hagar gone? Hasn't he? Fuzzy Duck? Does he? Ducky Fuzz? Maybe he has. Maybe he hasn't. The exact timings don't matter. What matters is how we all feel. How does he feel? How do I feel? How do the kids feel?

Everyone has their way of handling their life and we have ours. Hagar and I have always agreed that there will be no big goodbyes. Just business as usual. To us this is business as usual.

From my perspective, I have one life and I want to live it to the full. I can't waste energy I can't spare on things I can't control. I can't control what happens in Afghanistan and I can't worry about what I can't control. 'Que sera sera', sang Doris. Hagar knows his onions. He will be the best he can be. He knows what is at stake. He said to his guys; 'success to me is that we come back with as many as we go out with'.

The Chinook is an army asset. It is a tool, used to help the boots on the ground get the job done. Hagar knows he is there to support the guys on the ground, to achieve the task, to mitigate the risk and deliver the unthinkable. This is the job. This is his job.

What do I think? I want him to be vigilant at all times; to come home again. It is tiring though being strong, putting your head down, digging in and pushing through – again and again and again and again and again. I can't sit still, rocking under the table waiting for him to come home. We all have a life to live. A life to celebrate, so, I think I am just going to work, dance and drink through it and keep my kids smiling. I'll tell them that daddy is at work and when they say; "I miss daddy." I'll smile and say, "I miss daddy too. It's fine to miss daddy, but he has a job to do so that he can buy you toys." When you are 8 years old, saying food and keeping a roof over your head, keeping you safe at night doesn't have the same meaning as toys. Toys are an 8-year-old's currency. (Before we get into a materialism debate – The Grenade has a real sense of kindness, helpfulness, manners and solid values. But he loves toys).

We don't make a thing of it to the kids. Daddy is away. They don't know where he has gone or what he is doing. This is just normal. Daddy's here sometimes and sometimes he's not; that's just the way it is. I have said before there is a lot of away – exercises, night flying, day flying, practising – sometimes for a few days, sometimes for a few weeks, sometimes a few months. Away is just away. My kids deserve a childhood free of anxiety wherever possible. I believe that my job is to protect them from the reality of war and give them a carefree childhood full of love and possibilities. They will have adulthood to contend with eventually.

When he returns from war he has another battle to face in court.

Tick, tock, tick, tock – the clock ticks. Time passes and the war continues. To stay or go? If we stay there will be trouble. If we go there will be double.

To be continued...

Printed in Great Britain
by Amazon.co.uk, Ltd.,
Marston Gate.